Coffee and sunshine on a spring morning

Celia Latty-Steele

Presentation by *BookLeaf Publishing*

Web: www.bookleafpub.com

E-mail: info@bookleafpub.com

ISBN: 9789357616461

First edition 2022

Marnie - here's mine

She hasn't changed

The years have passed since we first met
But my friend, she hasn't changed

My health has waned, my spirit bent
But my friend, she hasn't changed

My eyes grow tired, my shoulders weary
But my friend, she hasn't changed

Thank God for my rock, my one constant
My friend, she hasn't changed

Let it come

Let it come upon you
Like the moon upon the night
Let it steal beside you
And sit close in your heart

Do not try to force it
Don't push to fit it in
It will happen in its moment
And the magic will begin

I know you want it straight away
You want it here and now
But slowly is the best way
My love, just let it come

I just can't let you go

You left us so completely, so suddenly that
heartbreaking night
We didn't get a real goodbye, couldn't hold you
one last time

Did you hear our prayers for you, our words of
love and hope
Did you hear us say you can go now, though we
wished for anything but?

The years without you are rolling by, as are the
tears down our cheeks
And I still have your clothes in my drawers, I
just can't let them go

I can't feel your hugs or hear your laugh
Can't ask you your advice
I know you are still guiding me but I just can't
let you go

Until I see you again I'm just going to pretend
You are just up ahead
Just around the next bend

The yellow jumper

I packed it away for another season, and the memories came flooding back

It's older now, stretched and worn but I can still feel it's warmth.

It's morning walks along the beach with a brand new puppy

Late night feeds with a brand new baby

It's football ovals and netball courts

Vet visits with an older dog when it was time to say goodbye

First day of school and last day of holidays

Its holding your Dad without realising it is the last time

It's love and it's heartbreak and every memory between

And I can't wait to see what the next season
brings

Mirabooka

Your beauty calmed me, soothed me and
embraced me

It captured my heart and soul and rocked me to
sleep at night

The roos came to meet me at twilight and the
birds sung their lullabies

The air you provided refreshed me and your
trees rejuvenated me

You were exactly what I needed at this exact
moment - thank you

Hope

I fought for you
I fought my body for you
I fought my mind for you
I fought heartache and desperation for you
I fought society for you
I fought how I thought my life would be for you
I will always fight for you

When you need me I will run to you
When I cannot run I will walk to you
When I cannot walk I will crawl
When I am no longer here, I will be around

You are my Hope, my joy and my life

Penpals

Flying through the air
We send our words
To different countries
To different worlds

We share our news
Our stories and dreams
Strangers become friends
The warmth just gleams

I thank you for being there
For being open, being free
Your letters have changed my life
You've allowed me to be me

Afternoon nap

The feeling of surrender is glorious

Close your eyes and breathe

Your body and soul needs this

Lie for a while in the cool room, in the quiet bed
and sleep

Coffee in the morning

I need you
Like the sun needs to rise
Like the tide needs to turn

I need you
You are there for me as I open my eyes
I stumble to the kitchen
You join my cup

You start my day
I walk outside and sit in the early sun, the chill
still on my shoulders
And drink in your magic

Books

My constant companion that never lets me down
A friend or distraction from this world that is
sometimes so hard

You have provided warmth and joy since I could
form the words
I will always be grateful for the gifts you have
given me

Adelaide

My city that has loved me
That's kept me safe for years
I thank you my dear Adelaide
I weep with happy tears

From the beaches that cool me down
To the wineries that warm me up
To the workplace I hold dearly
You always fill my cup

My love for you is everlasting
I've never wandered far
You hold me captivated
You are my shining star

The stage

You embrace me
You are my home
Where I am someone else
Many other people!

You have brought me joy
You have brought me stress
You have even brought me a husband!

I've not visited for a while
But I will
You have my heart
And I'll be back soon

Tiredness

The tiredness overwhelms me
It creeps over and swallows me

It sends its tentacles to cover me
It's darkness to envelope me

I want it to be gone, to beat it for good
I want to be the woman I was, once upon a time

It goes to sleep for a while
But it's always hovering
Waiting to drag me back

Walking at night

At night when I can't sleep I walk

I walk my neighbourhood streets

I walk the foreshore in Stansbury

I walk my favourite trail in the National park

I walk the city I used to live in London

I walk with my Dad, my old dog, my favourite authors

When I close my eyes, I can walk anywhere

Christmas through a child's eyes

The memories I hold have dimmed
But my girl, she brings it alive
The joy and simple love of Christmas
The experience through her eyes

Her love of Santa, of reindeer and presents
Her wonder at Jesus and what he gives
The lights that shine in the darkness
The experience through her eyes

I want it to be there forever
I'll hold it while I can
The love she shows for the season
The experience through her eyes

Dogs

We brought them home
When they had none
We gave them love, and shelter
But they gave us more

More than we ever expected or deserved
Their trust and comfort, when we needed them -
they were our family

They left us all too soon, but when would have
been right?
We will never forget the joy they brought to our
lives

Daddy's girl

She opens her eyes in the morning and calls for you

She wakes in the night and cries for you

She stops what she is doing and asks for you

She sees you come home and runs to you

She is her daddy's girl

Breakfast with Carly

When I'm low she seems to know
And a message she will send
It may be months but time means nothing
When it comes to my dear friend

She picks me up, she takes me out
She listens to my woes
In her easy way, no matter the distance
Up and off she goes

I want to thank you Carly
For everything you do
I am so very grateful
For having a friend like you

The river walk

The birds welcome me as old friends as I leave
my car
I breathe in the air and as it fills my lungs the
world feels right
As I start the trail I embrace the stillness in the
early morning
The traffic noise is a memory as I walk along its
paths

The river meanders along its way and I follow
I can leave my problems behind and appreciate
the beauty
The rawness of the weeds, the dirt under my
shoes
The smell of the water and the stories it hides

Runners pass me and dogs take their owners for
walks
We smile but continue our paths
The day may unravel before me but now
Now I'm at peace

Moving house

The time has come
To pack up the house

The place where we started our journey
The shell which held our hopes and dreams
Saw joys and devastating heartache
Its time to say goodbye

We have outgrown our little nest
We have certainly tried to make it fit
But now we have one too many for this old soul

So we pack the cupboards and empty the walls
Sweep the floors and cut the lawns
And hope for a new life for this place in which
we started ours

Gratitude

My life is sad, at times and hard
But I am grateful
It's not worked out quite how I planned
But I am grateful
For my love and my family
For my friends and my life
For the air I breathe and the freedoms I enjoy
I am grateful